KETO VEGAN

Essential Guide to Healthy Lifestyle and Easy Weight Loss;

With 70 Proven, Simple and Delicious Vegetarian Ketogenic Recipes

Second Edition

AUTHOR: JENNIFER MARTINS

Legal & Disclaimer

The information contained in this book and its contents is not designed to replace or take the place of any form of medical or professional advice; and is not meant to replace the need for independent medical, financial, legal or other professional advice or services, as may be required. The content and information in this book have been provided for educational and entertainment purposes only.

The content and information contained in this book have been compiled from sources deemed reliable, and it is accurate to the best of the Author's knowledge, information, and belief. However, the Author cannot guarantee its accuracy and validity and cannot be held liable for any errors and omissions. Further, changes are periodically made to this book as and when needed. Where appropriate and necessary, you must consult a professional (including but not limited to your doctor, attorney, financial advisor or such other professional advisor) before using any of the suggested remedies, techniques, or information in this book.

Upon using the contents and information contained in this book, you agree to hold harmless the Author from

Contents

Introduction

Our world is flawed; there is no doubt about that. However, there are various ways through which individuals can contribute to make this world a slightly better place for humans and other animals alike.

That being said, perhaps one of the most important issues that are plaguing the heart of our world are the sufferings of animals, proper maintenance of our personal health and climate change!

Believe it or not, a Vegan Diet addresses all of these issues with ease! Or, that is at least what people normally believe.

However, a Vegan diet alone won't be able to address all the health issues that may plague a human being!

There are some people who tend to stay much healthier when on a low-carb diet such as Ketogenic Diet while others tend to slow down on the high-carb vegan diet.

But here's the thing, as mentioned earlier a complete Vegan Diet might not be the best option for every health issue. For example, people with various conditions such as Parkinson's disease, Epilepsy, and Obesity, etc. can be helped a Ketogenic Diet much more when compared to a simple Vegan Diet.

But does that mean that you are supposed to forget all the ethical concerns of this world and break your Vegan diet? Not really!

Simply combine both of the diets to get the benefits of both of them!

That being said let me walk you through the necessary concepts that are required for the diet one by one.

First up!

Chapter 1: The Fundamentals of Ketogenic Diet

What does ketogenic diet mean?

The very first thing that comes to mind when talking about the ketogenic diet is that you should understand the meaning of *keto*.

This is a prefix that derives from a human metabolic process known as *ketosis*, which helps the body to process and produces chemicals known as *ketones*.

The main objective of a ketogenic diet is simply to lower the intake of carbohydrates to encourage the production of ketones.

How does a ketogenic diet work?

The working mechanism of a ketogenic diet might be slightly complex to absolute newcomers, but I will try my very best to simplify the whole process as much as possible.

But before you are able to fully appreciate and understand the process of a ketogenic diet, you must first learn to accept the fact that whenever our body is exposed to a large amount of carbohydrates, it tends to exponentially increase the production of glucose and insulin.

Glucose is quite possibly the most easily convertible molecule in our bodies, and whenever we are doing something that requires energy, our bodies rapidly break down glucose and convert it into chemical energy.

Insulin, on the other hand, helps to maintain the level of glucose in our bloodstream. Whenever the level of glucose gets too high, the production of insulin is increased, which lowers the glucose to safe levels.

But here's the thing, whenever glucose is abundantly present in our body, it also significantly decreases the amount of fat that is burned through workout or dieting, since the body burns the reserved glucose instead of the fat.

This is a very important and rather unknown reason why some people work out really hard but ultimately get no result. And this is where the ketogenic diet comes in.

Whenever your body is deprived of carbohydrates, it slowly starts to enter a state known as ketosis. This is, generally speaking, the body's natural response mechanism when it comes to dealing with low food intake.

Understanding the fundamentals of ketosis

I have already mentioned that the main objective of a keto diet is to restrict your carbs intake and encourage your body to enter ketosis, right?

Now let me explain what exactly this ketosis is. Simply put, whenever you are depriving your body of carbohydrates, it tends to start burning fat for energy instead of the carbohydrates.

This process is accelerated further due to the release of chemicals known as ketones, which encourage the body to break down fat instead of glucose.

This whole process is known as ketosis, and this process is at the heart of a ketogenic diet.

The signs and symptoms that you are in ketosis

I believe that you have a good understanding of ketosis, but it is essential that you properly understand the signs and symptoms that will help you assess whether your body is indeed in ketosis.

And you know what? It is really easy! Just be aware of the following signs:

- Your mouth will feel dry, and you feel increased thirst.
- The number of washroom visits will increase as you might need to urinate more often.
- Your breath will have a slight "fruity" smell that will resemble that of nail polish.
- Aside from those three, you will have a low hunger level and increased bodily energy.
- You may keep track of your ketosis by using urine strips (acetoacetate) and observing the color change. A darker purple means your body is rich in ketones.

How to maximize ketosis

Now you can obviously enter into a state of ketosis just by lowering your carb intake. However, there are always better ways of doing the same thing, right?

Following the steps below, you will prolong the period that your body stays in ketosis, thereby increasing the effectiveness of your ketogenic diet.

- Keep your daily carbohydrate intake below 20g.
- Keep your protein levels at around 70g per day.
- Don't starve! Consume adequate levels of fat. Remember that the body is going to need fat to burn.
- Try to avoid snacks and stick to your breakfast, lunch, and dinner meals with nothing in between.

Advantages of a ketogenic diet

So, now I will let you know a bit about the different advantages and benefits of going on a ketogenic diet!

- ✓ A properly planned and fixed ketogenic diet will allow your body to significantly lower the amount of bad cholesterol, which will later contribute to cleansing your body and preventing arterial blockages.
- ✓ Given the fact that fat is pretty much available everywhere in our body, once the body starts to burn fat to produce the required energy, it tends to be much more energetic due to the availability of fat.
- ✓ The body will become resistant to Type-2 diabetes, as following the ketogenic diet will result in a significant reduction of available LDL in the body.
- ✓ You won't always feel hungry.
- ✓ While your body is under ketosis, it improves the general condition of the skin and decreases the possibility of experiencing skin inflammation and various other problems such as acne.

Asides from these core benefits, you should know that the keto diet also contributes greatly when it comes to trimming excess body fat.

- • The diet will greatly improve the efficacy of workouts and generally enhance the amount of burned fat through day-to-day activities.

- During a keto diet, your body is forced to consume a greater amount of protein. This high protein consumption also leads to weight loss.
- Once you have cut off your high carb intake, your body starts to habituate itself to the new change, which will cause it to decrease the calories it processes as well. This will further help to trim down unwanted fat.
- While on a ketogenic diet, gluconeogenesis will slowly start to take place inside your body, which will accelerate the fat-burning as well.
- A ketogenic diet will allow you to have extreme control over your food craving and will allow you to control and suppress your hunger.

How a Keto Diet Will Help You Lose Weight

This is perhaps one of the main reasons why you have purchased this book in the first place! You want to lose those excess pounds, right?

Well, here is how it goes.

Whenever you eat a lot of carbohydrates, the body starts to burn those carbohydrates to produce energy for the body, and it stores the excess as triglycerides.

When carbohydrates are taken out of this whole equation, the glycogen stores in the liver and muscle eventually burn out, after which the body starts to obtain energy from fat.

Not only does the body start to burn the fat you eat, but it also starts to burn the triglycerides stored in your fatty cells.

All of these effects together result in your body shrinking the fat cells, eventually making you leaner and less obese.

Some physical effects to keep in mind

With such a drastic change in your diet, your body is bound to experience some physical changes in your overall homeostatic functions.

Eventually, the body will start to habituate itself to the type of meals that you are taking in by producing more enzymes to digest those particular types of meals easily.

During the early stage of your diet, some minor side effects that you might experience include:

- Dizziness
- Aggravation
- Headaches
- Keto "flu"
- Mental fogginess

Aside from those, some symptoms that you should be aware of are:

- **Frequent desire to urinate:** Since ketosis will cause your body to burn up more fat, the glycogen gets stored up. In this situation, your kidneys will start to process a lot of water to excrete it, increasing your desire to urinate.
- **Hypoglycemia:** This simply means that your sugar level might drop.
- **Constipation:** This is yet another side effect experienced by some that take place due to

dehydration and lower salt in the body. But this can very easily be tackled by drinking more water.

- **Increased sugar craving:** During the early stages of your diet, you might get a serious craving for sugar. To tackle this, simply take some extra protein and Vitamin B-complex. A good and healthy walk works well too.
- **Diarrhea:** This is a common issue faced by some people at the beginning, but it resolves itself automatically after a few days.
- **Sleep problems:** This might be a result of the reduced levels of serotonin or insulin.

When the body is in a state of ketosis, it causes plenty of electrolytes to be flushed out from the body, which is the main reason for such effects taking place. This diuretic effect can be tackled by increasing the level of water consumption during a ketogenic diet. Other advice would be to increase your normal salt intake, which will also help to rejuvenate the levels of electrolytes.

So, keep in mind that if you are experiencing any of the symptoms mentioned above, they are pretty normal, and there is nothing to be worried!

Some healthy tips for a better journey

- Get yourself a carb counter to keep your daily carb intake in check.
- Make sure to get rid of all of your high-carb products from the cupboard.

- Slowly try to alter your daily habits and accept new ones to make sure that they will complement your new diet style.
- Try to stay as hydrated as you can by drinking water.
- Always make ensure adequate sodium intake. It will make your keto journey much more pleasant. Some tips include:
  - ✓ Take a just a pinch of pink salt with your meals.
  - ✓ Add a ¼ teaspoon of pink salt to 16 ounces of water.
  - ✓ Add vegetables such as kelp to your dishes.
  - ✓ Eat vegetables such as cucumber or celery for a more natural approach to sodium replenishment.
- Try to include a basic amount of physical exercise into your diet regimen as well. It will not only make you healthy but also accelerate the effectiveness of your keto diet. A general exercise routine may include:
  - ✓ Monday: Resistance training for upper body (20 minutes)
  - ✓ Tuesday: Resistance training for lower body (20 minutes)
  - ✓ Wednesday: 30-minute walk
  - ✓ Thursday: Resistance training for upper body (20 minutes)
  - ✓ Friday: Resistance training for lower body (20 minutes)
  - ✓ Sat/Sun: Recreational time.

With that we are done with the Ketogenic Part of our Diet, now let's focus on a vegan part.

Chapter 2: Understanding Vegan Diet and Linking it to a Keto Diet

The Vegan Ketogenic Diet is perhaps one of the more restrictive diets out there and maintaining all of the rules might be slightly difficult in the beginning. However, that is not to say that it is impossible!

The diet altogether won't only improve your health, but will also largely decrease animal cruelty and suffering!

But before going deeper, let me first discuss what the word "Vegan" actually means.

That being said, the following rules are to be implemented in order to fully link a Vegan Diet with a Ketogenic Diet!

The Meaning of "Vegan"

Generally speaking, Vegan diet is a type of diet that encourages an individual to exclude any and every kind of ingredients that are animal based.

That means asides from meat; eggs, milk and even cheese are completely off the table.

A person who follows a Vegan diet does not only follow it for the sake of staying healthy though! Veganism is nothing short of a lifestyle that encourages a revolution against animal cruelty and exploitation.

At this point, you should be aware that there is actually a considerable amount of difference between Veganism and Vegetarianism.

The people who follow a Vegan diet often tend to consider themselves as being children of nature, and they appreciate whatever Mother Nature has to offer.

As mentioned before, individuals who follow a Vegan diet tend to completely restrict themselves from having any kind of animal/dairy products or anything that is even remotely related to animals.

On the other hand, Vegetarians allow a degree of freedom in this matter by allowing animal-derived products such as milk or eggs.

The Required Rules for Keto Vegan Diet

- Make sure to limit your daily carbohydrate intake to less than 35g

- Make sure to eliminate all kinds of meat, including fish

- Since this is a vegan based diet, no animal-derived products are allowed as well

- Make sure to go for plenty of low-carb veggies

- Make sure to get at least 70% of your calories from plant-based fats

- Make sure to get about 25% of your daily calories from plant-based proteins

- To make sure that your body is getting all minerals, vitamin, and nutrients, you are to go for some supplements as well (I will discuss that later in the subsequent chapter)

Learn how to Limit Your Carbs While on a Keto Vegan Diet

Maintaining a restricted carb intake while on a normal Ketogenic diet is difficult enough! So naturally, you might think that it might be even difficult to maintain your carb intake while on a Vegan diet right?

Well, let me give you some guidelines to make the process that much easier!

That being said,

These are...

The Ingredients to avoid:

- Grains such as wheat, rice, cereal, corn, etc.
- Legumes such as black beans, peas, and lentils
- Sugar including maple syrup, agave, and honey
- Fruits that are high in sugar such as orange, bananas, and apple
- Tubers such as Yams and Potatoes

And these are...

The ones to go for:

- Vegan meats such as tofu, tempeh, Seitan and other high-Protein and low carb Vegan meats
- Mushrooms
- Vegetables that grow above ground such as broccoli, zucchini, and cauliflower, etc.

- Leafy greens such as kale and spinach

- High-Fat Vegan dairy such as vegan cheese, coconut cream, unsweetened coconut-based yogurt, etc.

- Nuts and Seeds such as sunflower seeds, pistachio, almonds, etc.

- Avocado and berries such as raspberries, blackberries,

- Fermented food such as Natto, Kim Chi, and Sauerkraut and so on.

- Sea veggies such as bladderwrack, dulse, etc.

- Sweeteners such as monk fruit, Stevia, Erythritol, etc.

- Fats such as coconut oil, red palm oil, olive oil and MCT oil

By following the ingredients listed under "Go For", you will be able to easily follow a vegan Keto diet that will cover up most of your nutritional needs.

But let me dive into the matter a little bit more.

The Vegan Alternatives

There are various Ketogenic Recipes that call for non-vegan ingredients such as eggs, cheese and so on.

While the recipes in this book will provide you with a nice foundation of what kind of meals you should follow, the following list will give you some very simple alternatives to Non-Vegan ingredients that will allow you to convert any Keto Recipe into a Keto Vegan one!

- If the recipe calls for Milk, replace it with coconut milk
- If the recipe calls for Heavy Cream, replace it with Coconut Cream
- Try to use Coconut oil or Vegan Butter instead of Butter
- Replace your Dairy-Based cheese with Vegan Cheese
- Try to use Vegan Soft Cheese instead of Cream Cheese
- Replace your yogurt with sour cream or other nut-based yogurts

The Egg Replacers

Honestly speaking, it is rather frustrating to see that most mouthwatering Keto recipes call for eggs!

Does that mean you hope and dreams are over?

Not really!

Here are some amazing alternatives that can be used to replace your Eggs and further help you to Veganize the Keto meals!

- Flax Seed
- Silken Tofu
- Baking Soda

Oils to Provide You With Enough Fat

As mentioned earlier, it is important that you take in a good amount of Fat while you are on a Ketogenic Vegan diet, since otherwise, it will hamper the normal working condition of your body.

The following oils will help you to stay in line

- Coconut oil
- Olive Oil
- Avocado Oil
- Red Palm Oil
- MCT Oil
- Nuts
- Seeds
- Vegan Dairy Substitute

Now to Cover Your Protein!

Similar to fat, a Keto Vegan diet will also require you to maintain appropriate levels of protein intake to ensure that things are going well!

Therefore, the following ingredients are to be kept in mind

- Tofu
- Seitan
- Nuts and Seeds
- Vegan Protein Powder

If you feel that you require additional protein for your body, feel free to add vegan protein powder in your food or juices or smoothies (some of the plant-based protein powder are hemp protein powder, pumpkin protein powder, cranberry protein powder, and so on).

A Note on Your Vitamin Supplements

As mentioned earlier, while you are on a Keto-Vegan diet, there's a possibility that you might face some vitamin or mineral deficiency, to keep yourself free form such problems! Keep the following supplements within reach.

Just to be clear, always make sure to consult with your physician before adding any supplements to your daily diet.

- **Vitamin B12:** Try to take supplements that contain B12 in cyanocobalamin form for maximum effectiveness.

- **Vitamin D:** Go for D2 or Vegan D3 that are manufactured by Viridian or Nordic Naturals.
- **EPA and DHA:** Take from algae oil.
- **Iron:** Should only be ingested using supplements should you face deficiency. Otherwise, avoid taking extra Iron.
- **Iodine:** Either take supplements or add ½ a teaspoon of iodized salt to your daily diet.
- **Calcium:** Take tablets of 500mg or less daily.
- **Zinc:** Take in forms of Zinc Citrate or Zinc Gluconate. Make sure that you are not to take these while taking Calcium supplements.

Chapter 3: Breakfast Recipes

Fresh Avocado and Cilantro Bowl

Prep Time: 10 minutes

Cooking Time: 0 minute

Serving: 6

Ingredients:

- 2 avocados – peeled, pitted and diced
- 1 chopped up a sweet onion
- 1 green bell pepper (chopped up)
- 1 large sized chopped up a ripe tomato
- ¼ cup of chopped up fresh cilantro
- ½ of a juiced lime
- Salt as needed
- Pepper as needed

Directions:

1. Take a medium-sized bowl and add the avocados, onion, tomato, bell pepper, cilantro and lime juice

2. Give the whole mixture a nice toss to ensure that everything is coated well with the juice

3. Season with some additional salt and pepper if needed

4. Enjoy!

Nutrition Values (Per Serving)

- Calories: 126
- Fat: 10g
- Carbohydrates: 10g
- Protein: 2.1g

The Low and Slow Creamy Broccoli Soup

Serving: 2

Prep Time: 5 minutes

Cook Time: 30 minutes

Ingredients

- 1 can of full-fat coconut milk
- 3 cups of chopped celery
- 3 cups of chopped broccoli florets
- 2 cups of vegetable stock
- ½ a teaspoon of onion powder
- ½ a teaspoon of garlic pepper
- Salt as needed
- Pepper as needed
- Red pepper flakes as needed

How To

1. Take a pot and place it over medium heat
2. Add the ingredients to the pot and cook for about 30 minutes until the broccoli and celery are tender
3. Transfer the soup to a blender and process them until smooth
4. Enjoy the hot soup!

Nutrition Values (Per Serving)

- Calories: 200
- Fat: 17g
- Carbs: 5g
- Protein: 4g

The Low Carb Vegan "Pumpkin Risotto"

Serving: 8

Prep Time: 10 minutes

Cook Time: 20 minutes

Ingredients

- ¼ cup of sliced leek
- 2 tablespoon of Olive oil
- 1 teaspoon of paprika
- 12 ounce of riced cauliflower
- ½ a cup of pureed pumpkin
- ¼ cup of nutritional yeast
- ¼ cup of vegetable broth
- Salt as needed
- Pepper as needed
- ¼ cup of fresh chopped up parsley

How To

1. Take a large sized frying pan and place it over medium heat
2. Add olive oil, paprika, leek, salt and pepper
3. Allow the leek to soften while stirring it constantly
4. Add cauliflower rice and stir until it is well mixed
5. Pour the vegetable broth and place lid, cook for 10-15 minutes until the cauliflower do not stick
6. Stir in pumpkin puree and nutritional yeast
7. Stir well and taste, making sure to season it with some more salt and pepper if needed
8. Garnish with some parsley and serve!

Nutrition Values (Per Serving)

- Calories: 126
- Fat: 8g
- Carbs: 10g
- Protein: 6g

Avocado Spread

Serves: 4

Prep Time: 10 minutes

Cook Time: 0 minutes

Ingredients

- 1 halved and pitted avocado
- 2 tablespoon of chopped fresh parsley
- 1 and a ½ teaspoon of extra virgin olive oil
- ½ a lemon juice
- ½ a teaspoon of salt
- ½ a teaspoon of ground black pepper
- ½ a teaspoon of onion powder
- ½ a teaspoon of garlic powder

Directions

1. Scoop out the avocado flesh into a bowl
2. Add lemon juice, parsley, olive oil, salt, onion powder, garlic, and pepper
3. Mix well and mash the mixture using a potato masher
4. Serve the avocado spread as you like
5. Enjoy!

Nutritional Values per Serving

- Calories: 170
- Fat: 12g
- Carbohydrates: 11g
- Protein: 5g

Very Fine Cabbage Slaw

Serving: 8

Prep Time: 10 minutes

Cook Time: 0 minutes

Ingredients

For Salad

- 2 cups of shredded red cabbage
- 2 cups of shredded green cabbage
- 2 thinly sliced scallions
- ¼ cup of shredded carrots
- 2 tablespoon of sesame seeds

For dressing

- 1 tablespoon of rice wine vinegar
- 1 tablespoon of tamari
- 1 tablespoon of sesame oil
- ½ a teaspoon of grated ginger

- ½ a teaspoon of minced garlic

How To

1. Take a bowl and add all of the dressing ingredients
2. Whisk them well and keep it on the side to allow the flavors to incorporate
3. Take a large sized serving bowl and add cabbage, carrots, scallions and combine
4. Toss the veggies with the dressing and sprinkle sesame seeds on top
5. Enjoy!

Nutrition Values (Per Serving)

- Calories: 84
- Fat: 5g
- Carbs: 4g
- Protein: 2g

Astonishing Vegan Hemp Seed Yogurt

Serving: 8

Prep Time: 200 minutes

Cook Time: 0 minutes

Ingredients

- ¾ cup of hulled hemp seeds
- 3 cups of boiling water
- ¼ cup of lemon juice
- 2 teaspoon of xanthan gum
- Stevia as needed

How To

1. Take a pan and bring water to a boil
2. Take 1 cup of boiling water and mix them with hemp seeds in a blender
3. Process until the smooth lump-free mixture forms
4. While the blender is still processing, add xanthan gum and 2 cups of remaining water

5. Process for 30 seconds more
6. Add lemon juice and blend for a little longer
7. Pour into a container and allow it to chill for 2-3 hours
8. Once the yogurt has set, enjoy!

Nutrition Values (Per Serving)

- Calories: 166
- Fat: 12g
- Carbs: 4g
- Protein: 10g

Sensual Portobello Mushrooms

Prep Time: 10 minutes

Cooking Time: 10 minutes

Serving: 2

Ingredients:

- 2 Portobello mushrooms
- ½ cup of extra virgin olive oil
- 2 tablespoons of chopped onion
- 3 minced clove of garlic
- 3 tablespoons of balsamic vinegar

Directions:

1. Carefully clear up mushrooms and remove stems
2. Keep the mushrooms for later use
3. Place the caps on a plate (gills upward)

4. Take a small sized bowl and add onion, vinegar, oil, and garlic
5. Mix everything well
6. Pour the mixture over the mushrooms caps and allow it to stand for about 60 minutes
7. Grill for about 10 minutes over your grill
8. Enjoy the grilled Portobello Mushrooms!

Nutrition Values (Per Serving)

- Calories: 177
- Fat: 14
- Carbohydrates: 7
- Protein: 2.4g

Surprisingly Keto Tomato Tart

Serving: 8

Prep Time: 10 minutes

Cook Time: 25 minutes

Ingredients

For Crust

- ½ a cup of coconut oil
- ¾ cup of coconut flour
- ½ a teaspoon of salt
- the mixture of 1 tablespoon of ground flaxseed + ¼ cup of water

For Filling

- 4 ounce of heirloom tomatoes

- 3 ounce of vegan cheese substitute
- Black pepper and other herbs as needed

How To

1. Pre-heat your oven to 350 degrees Fahrenheit
2. Take a 9-inches pan and add all of the crust ingredients
3. Spread them out evenly and bake for 15-20 minutes until the crust starts to set
4. Remove the crust
5. Spread the vegan cheese shredded over the crust
6. Slice up tomatoes into ¼ inch slices and arrange them on top of the Cheese
7. Sprinkle cracked pepper, oregano, basil and any other herbs of your choice
8. Cover and bake for 20-25 minutes until the cheese has melted, and the tomatoes are tender
9. Allow it to cool and enjoy!

Nutrition Values (Per Serving)

- Calories: 212
- Fat: 18g
- Carbs: 5g
- Protein: 2g

Kalamata Olive Tapenade

Prep Time: 15 minutes

Cooking Time: 0 minute

Serving: 4

Ingredients:

- 3 peeled garlic cloves
- 1 cup of pitted kalamata olives
- 2 tablespoons of capers
- 3 tablespoons of chopped fresh parsley
- 2 tablespoons of lemon juice
- 2 tablespoons of extra virgin olive oil
- Salt as needed
- Pepper as needed

Directions:

1. Take a food processor and add garlic cloves
2. Pulse them well until they are fully minced
3. Add olives, olive oil, capers, parsley, lemon juice to the food processor and blend them well until the whole mixture is finely chopped up

4. Season with some pepper and salt
- Serve and enjoy!

Nutrition Values (Per Serving)

- Calories: 81
- Fat: 8g
- Carbohydrates: 3g
- Protein: 0.5g

Silly Scallion Pancakes

Serving: 4

Prep Time: 5 minutes

Cook Time: 10 minutes

<u>Ingredients</u>

For Cakes

- ½ a cup of coconut flour
- 2 tablespoon of Psyllium Husk powder
- ½ a teaspoon of garlic powder
- ¼ teaspoon of salt
- 2-3 scallions sliced up into thin portions
- ¼ cup of sesame oil
- 1 cup of warm water

For Sauce

- 1 tablespoon of tamari sauce

- 1 teaspoon of rice wine vinegar
- 1 tablespoon of water
- 1 teaspoon of sesame oil
- 1 finely minced garlic clove
- Chili flakes as needed

How To

1. Take a frying pan and place it over medium-low heat
2. Add sesame oil and heat it up
3. Take a mixing bowl and add water, oil, garlic, salt, scallions, warm water and allow it to stand for 5 minutes to allow the flavors to mix up
4. Take another bowl and add coconut flour and the Psyllium Husk
5. Gently add the water to the dry ingredients, making sure to mix it well until the dough forms
6. Separate the dough into individual balls and flatten the balls into 4-inch rounds
7. Place the rounds in your skillet and fry for 5 minutes each side until they are golden
8. Keep repeating until the balls are used up
9. Enjoy!

Nutrition Values (Per Serving)

- Calories: 206
- Fat: 16g
- Carbs: 4g
- Protein: 4g

The Keto Crack Slaw

Serving: 2

Prep Time: 5 minutes

Cook Time: 10 minutes

Ingredients

- 4 cups of shredded green cabbage
- ½ a cup of macadamia nuts chopped up
- 1 teaspoon of chili paste
- 1 teaspoon of vinegar
- 2 tablespoon of tamari
- 1 tablespoon of sesame oil
- 2 garlic cloves
- Sesame seeds as needed

How To

1. Take a pan and place it over medium-low heat and add tamari, sesame oil, vinegar, sesame oil and chili paste

2. Add your green cabbage
3. Cover and allow it to cook for 5 minutes until the cabbage starts to tender
4. Stir everything and combine them well
5. Add the nuts
6. Cook for 5 minutes more until the nuts are tender
7. Serve and garnish
8. Enjoy!

Nutrition Values (Per Serving)

- Calories: 360
- Fat: 33g
- Carbs: 7g
- Protein: 7g

Feisty Grilled Artichokes

Prep Time: 5 minutes

Cooking Time: 30 minute

Serving: 4

Ingredients:

- 2 large sized artichokes
- 1 quartered lemon
- ¾ cup of extra virgin olive oil
- 4 chopped up garlic cloves
- 1 teaspoon of salt
- ½ a teaspoon of ground black pepper

Directions:

1. Take a large sized bowl and fill it up with cold water

2. Squeeze a bit of lemon juice from the wedges

3. Trim the upper part of your chokes, making sure to trim any damaged leaves as well

4. Cut the chokes up in half lengthwise portions

5. Add the chokes to your bowl of lemon water

6. Bring the whole pot to a boil

7. Pre-heat your outdoor grill to about medium-high heat

8. Allow the chokes to cook in the boiling pot for 15 minutes

9. Drain the chokes and keep them on the side

10. Take another medium-sized bowl and squeeze the remaining lemon

11. Stir in garlic and olive to the lemon mix

12. Brush up the chokes with the garlic dip and place them on your pre-heated grill

13. Grill for about 10 minutes, making sure to keep basting them until the edges are just slightly charred

14. Serve with the dip and enjoy!

Nutrition Values (Per Serving)

- Calories: 402
- Fat: 40g
- Carbohydrates: 10g
- Protein: 2.9g

The Thundering Cinnamon Chocolate Smoothie

Serving: 1

Prep Time: 5 minutes

Cook Time: 0 minutes

Ingredients

- ¾ cup of coconut milk
- ½ of a ripe avocado
- 2 teaspoon of unsweetened cocoa powder
- 1 teaspoon of cinnamon powder
- ¼ teaspoon of vanilla extract
- Stevia as needed
- ½ a teaspoon of coconut oil

How To

1. Add all of the ingredients to your blender and blend well until smooth

2. Allow them it to chill and enjoy!

Nutrition Values (Per Serving)

- Calories: 300
- Fat: 30g
- Carbs: 14g
- Protein: 5g

Vegan Enchilada Macaroni

Serving: 4

Prep Time: 20 minutes

Cook Time: 45 minutes

Ingredients

For Sauce

- 1 cup of hemp seeds
- ½ a cup of nutritional yeast
- ¼ cup of sliced red, yellow or orange bell peppers
- ½ a teaspoon of salt
- ½ a teaspoon of onion powder
- ½ a cup of water

For The Main Recipe

- 2 pack of Shirataki macaroni (Tofu)
- 1 can of young, green jackfruit in brine
- ¼ cup of enchilada sauce

How To

1. Pre-heat your oven to a temperature of 350 degrees Fahrenheit
2. Drain and chop up your jackfruit with a knife and add 2 tablespoons of enchilada sauce, toss them well.
3. Keep it on the side
4. Blend the sauce ingredients in a blender and process them well
5. Drain and rinse the noodles thoroughly and transfer them to a baking dish
6. Add sauce, jackfruit to the baking dish and mix well
7. Bake for 45 minutes
8. Allow it to cool and enjoy!

Nutrition Values (Per Serving)

- Calories: 192
- Fat: 7.4g
- Carbs: 4.1g
- Protein: 9.6g

Squash Salad for the Green Lovers!

Prep Time: 15 minutes

Cooking Time: 30 minutes

Serving: 4

<u>Ingredients</u>:

- 2 tablespoons of extra virgin olive oil
- 1 small sized sliced onion
- 2 medium-sized coarsely chopped tomatoes
- 1 teaspoon of salt
- ¼ teaspoon of pepper
- 2 small zucchini cut up into ½ inch slices
- 2 small sized yellow summer squash cut up into ½ inch slices
- 1 bay leaf
- ½ a teaspoon of dried basil

Directions:

1. Take a skillet and place it over medium heat
2. Add oil and allow it to heat up
3. Add onions and stir-fry them for about 5 minutes
4. Add tomatoes to the pan and mix well
5. Season the mixture with salt and pepper
6. Keep stirring for about 5 minutes until nicely cooked
7. Add bay leaf, zucchini, yellow squash, and basil
8. Lower down the heat and allow it to simmer for about 20 minutes, making sure to keep stirring it occasionally
9. Discard the bay leaf and enjoy!

Nutrition Values (Per Serving)

- Calories: 65
- Fat:5g
- Carbohydrates: 5g
- Protein: 1.5g

Chapter 4: Lunch Recipes

Avocado and Cucumber Salad

Prep Time: 15 minutes

Cooking Time: 0 minute

Serving: 4

<u>Ingredients</u>:

- 2 medium-sized cubed cucumbers
- 2 cubed avocados
- 4 tablespoons of chopped up fresh cilantro
- 1 minced garlic clove
- 2 tablespoons of minced green onions
- ¼ teaspoon of salt
- Black pepper as needed
- ¼ large sized lemon
- 1 piece of lime

Directions:

1. Take a large-sized bowl and add cilantro, avocado, and cucumber
2. Stir in pepper, onion, garlic, and salt
3. Take a lemon and squeeze on top
4. Toss everything well
5. Allow it to chill for 30 minutes
6. Serve and enjoy!

Nutrition Values (Per Serving)

- Calories: 186
- Fat: 15g
- Carbohydrates: 11g
- Protein: 4.1g

Obligatory Yellow Squash

Prep Time: 10 minutes

Cooking Time: 10 minutes

Serving: 8

Ingredients:

- 4 medium-sized yellow squash
- ½ a cup of extra virgin olive oil
- 2 cloves of crushed garlic
- Salt as needed
- Pepper as needed

Directions:

1. Pre-heat your grill over medium heat
2. Cut up the squash into ¼ inch thick slices
3. Take a small sized pan and add olive oil
4. Heat it up
5. Add garlic cloves and cover it up

6. Cook over medium heat until the garlic starts to sizzle and a nice fragrant comes
7. Brush the slice of the squash with the garlic oil and season them with some salt and pepper
8. Grill the squash slices for about 10 minutes per sides until they reached the desired tenderness
9. Brush them up with some more garlic oil and enjoy!

Nutrition Values (Per Serving)

- Calories: 146
- Fat:14g
- Carbohydrates: 4g
- Protein: 1g

Smooth Chili Coconut and Cauliflower Rice

Serving: 3

Prep Time: 20 minutes

Cook Time: 20 minutes

Ingredients

- 3 cups of riced cauliflower
- 2/3 cup of full-fat coconut milk
- 1-2 teaspoon of sriracha paste
- ¼-1/2 a teaspoon of onion powder
- Salt as needed
- Fresh basil for garnish

How To

1. Take a pan and place it over medium-low heat

2. Add all of the ingredients and stir them until fully combined
3. Cook for about 5-10 minutes, making sure that the lid is on
4. Remove the lid and keep cooking until any excess liquid goes away
5. Once the rice is soft and creamy, enjoy!

Nutrition Values (Per Serving)

- Calories: 103
- Fat: 7g
- Carbs: 4g
- Protein: 3g

Surprisingly Epic Vegan Borscht

Serving: 4

Prep Time: 10 minutes

Cook Time: 15 minutes

Ingredients

- 1 cup of shredded beets
- ½ a cup of shredded carrots
- 2 cups of shredded green cabbage
- 3 cups of vegetable stock
- 2 tablespoon of olive oil
- 1-2 tablespoon of lemon juice
- ½ a teaspoon of onion powder
- ½ a teaspoon of garlic powder
- Salt as needed
- Pepper as needed

How To

1. Take a stock pot and place it over medium-low heat
2. Add the beets cabbage and carrots and Saute them in heated up olive oil
3. Ad seasoning alongside the vegetable stock
4. Allow it to simmer until the veggies are tender
5. Remove the heat and allow it to cool
6. Serve with some chopped up dill and vegan compliant sour cream

Nutrition Values (Per Serving)

- Calories: 95
- Fat: 7g
- Carbs: 6g
- Protein: 1g

The Happy Spaghetti Squash

Serving: 4

Prep Time: 10 minutes

Cook Time: 60 minutes

Ingredients

- 1 large sized spaghetti squash
- 2 tablespoon of olive oil
- 1 teaspoon of garlic powder
- 1 teaspoon of dried rosemary
- 1 teaspoon of dried thyme
- 1 teaspoon of dried parsley
- ½ a teaspoon of sage
- 1 teaspoon of salt
- ½ a teaspoon of cracked pepper

How To

1. Pre-heat your oven to 350 degrees Fahrenheit

2. Split the squash and scrape out seeds and place it face down in a roasting pan
3. Pour water into the bottom and steam your squash
4. Roast the squash in your oven for 45 minutes
5. Remove the squash and allow it to cool
6. Scrape the flesh with a fork and add salt, spices, and oil
7. Mix well
8. Return it to the oven and cook for 15 minutes more
9. Enjoy!

Nutrition Values (Per Serving)

- Calories: 91
- Fat: 7g
- Carbs: 5g
- Protein: 3g

Ever so Popular Lemon Eggplant

Prep Time: 15 minutes

Cooking Time: 25 minutes

Serving: 4

Ingredients:

- 1 large sized eggplant
- 3 tablespoons of extra virgin olive oil
- Salt as needed
- Pepper as needed
- 2 tablespoons of fresh lemon juice

Directions:

1. Pre-heat your oven to a temperature of 400 degrees Fahrenheit
2. Take a baking sheet and line it up with parchment paper
3. Slice up the eggplant into half-lengthwise and cut the halves into quarters

4. Cut up the halves into moons and add the prepared eggplants to your baking sheet
5. Make sure to keep the skin side facing down
6. Brush the eggplants with olive oil
7. Season with some pepper and salt
8. Roast the eggplants in the oven for 30 minutes until they are lightly browned
9. Remove and season with a bit of lemon juice
10. Serve and enjoy!

Nutrition Values (Per Serving)

- Calories: 120
- Fat: 10g
- Carbohydrates: 8g
- Protein: 1.2g

Mushroom Soup With Coconut Cream

Serving: 5

Prep Time: 0 minutes

Cook Time: 40 minutes

Ingredients

- 1 tablespoon of Olive Oil
- ½ of a large diced onion
- 20 ounce of sliced mushrooms
- 6 minced garlic cloves
- 2 cup of vegetable broth
- 1 cup of coconut cream
- 1 cup f coconut milk
- ¾ teaspoon of salt
- ¼ teaspoon of black pepper

How To

1. Take a large sized pot and place it over medium heat
2. Add onion and mushrooms in olive oil and Saute for 10-15 minutes
3. Make sure to keep stirring it from time to time until browned evenly
4. Add garlic and Saute for 10 minutes more
5. Add vegetable broth, coconut cream, coconut milk, black pepper, and salt
6. Bring it to a boil and lower down the temperature to low
7. Simmer for 15 minutes
8. Use an immersion blender to puree the mixture
9. Enjoy!

Nutrition Values (Per Serving)

- Calories: 229
- Fat: 21g
- Carbs: 8g
- Protein: 5g

Stinky Roasted Garlic

Serves: 2

Prep Time: 5 minutes

Cook Time: 20 minutes

Ingredients

- 2 medium garlic heads
- 2 tablespoon of olive oil

Directions

1. Pre-heat your oven to a temperature of 250 degrees Fahrenheit
2. Peel each of your garlic clove
3. Place the cloves in a single layer in a small sized baking dish and drizzle some olive oil
4. Bake for about 15 minutes until the garlic are tender

Nutritional Values per Serving

- Calories: 81
- Fat: 7g
- Carbohydrates: 5g
- Protein: 1g

The Crazy Tofu Bok Choy Salad

Serving: 5

Prep Time: 30 minutes

Cook Time: 30 minutes

Ingredients

Oven Baked Tofu

- 15 ounces of extra firm tofu
- 1 tablespoon of Tamari
- 1 tablespoon of sesame oil
- 1 tablespoon of water
- 2 teaspoon of minced garlic
- 1 tablespoon of rice wine vinegar
- ½ a lemon juice

Bok Choy Salad

- 9 ounces of Bok Choy
- 1 green onion stalk
- 2 tablespoon of chopped cilantro
- 3 tablespoon of coconut oil
- 2 tablespoon of Tamari
- 1 tablespoon of Sambal Olek
- 1 tablespoon of peanut butter
- Juice of ½ a lime
- 7 drops of liquid Stevia

How To

1. Press your tofu with heavy weight for 5 hours
2. Take a bowl and add all of the marinade ingredients - Tamari, water, sesame oil, garlic, lemon juice, and vinegar
3. Chop up the tofu into square pieces and place them in a bag alongside the marinade
4. Allow them to marinate for 30 minutes or overnight
5. Pre-heat your oven to 350 degrees Fahrenheit and place your tofu on a baking sheet lined up parchment paper
6. Bake for 30-35 minutes
7. Add all of the salad dressing mixtures except Bok Choy in a bowl and mix well
8. Add chopped up Bok Choy, toss well
9. Remove the tofu from your oven and assemble the salad by mixing the Bok Choy, Tofu, and Sauce
10. Enjoy!

Nutrition Values (Per Serving)

- Calories: 398
- Fat: 30g
- Carbs: 6g
- Protein: 24g

A Spicy Red Coconut Curry for Keto Vegans

Serving: 4

Prep Time: 10 minutes

Cook Time: 25 minutes

Ingredients

- 1 cup of broccoli florets
- 1 large sized handful of spinach
- 4 tablespoon of coconut oil
- ¼ medium onion
- 1 teaspoon of minced garlic
- 1 teaspoon of minced ginger
- 2 teaspoon of Tamari
- 1 tablespoon of red curry paste
- ½ a cup of coconut cream
- 2 teaspoon of special sauce

Special Sauce

- 1 and a ½ cup of shredded seaweed
- 6 cups of water

- 6 fat clove garlic crushed but not peeled
- 1 tablespoon of peppercorns
- 1 cup of mushroom Tamari
- 1 tablespoon of miso

How To

1. Take a large saucepan and add garlic, peppercorns, water and bring to a boil
2. Lower down heat and simmer for 20 minutes
3. Strain and return the liquid to the pot
4. Add Tamari and bring to a boil again and cook it is very salty
5. Remove the heat and stir in miso
6. This is your special sauce
7. Chop up your onion and mince garlic
8. Take a pan and place it over medium-high heat, add chopped up onions and minced garlic
9. Add two tablespoon of coconut oil and cook until translucent
10. Turn the heat down to medium-low and add broccoli to pan, stir well
11. Once the broccoli is cooked, move the veggies on the side and add curry paste
12. Cook for 60 seconds
13. Add spinach and top and cook until wilt, add coconut cream alongside the remaining coconut oil
14. Stir and add Tamari, special sauce, ginger and allow it to simmer for 10 minutes more
15. Enjoy!

Nutrition Values (Per Serving)

- Calories: 310
- Fat: 22g
- Carbs: 5g
- Protein: 25g

Quick and Easy Caesar Salad

Serving: 4

Prep Time: 10 minutes

Cook Time: 0 minutes

Ingredients

- 1 piece of ripe avocado
- 3 tablespoon of lemon juice
- 2 tablespoon of water
- 3 minced garlic minced up
- 1 tablespoon of caper brine
- 1 tablespoon of capers
- 2 teaspoon of Dijon mustard
- Sea salt as needed
- Pepper as needed
- ¼ cup of hemp seeds
- 12 cups of chopped up romaine leaves

How To

1. Take a bowl and add avocado, water, lemon juice, brine, garlic, capers, pepper and mustard salt
2. Add the contents to a blender and pulse until smooth
3. Add some water if your desired consistency is not reached
4. Spoon the dressing into a bowl
5. Add hemp seeds and mix
6. Add romaine lettuce to a large sized salad bowl and drop the dressing on top
7. Enjoy!

Nutrition Values (Per Serving)

- Calories: 281
- Fat: 24g
- Carbs: 12g
- Protein: 6g

Creamy Roasted Pepper Soup

Serving: 4

Prep Time: 0 minutes

Cook Time: 30 minutes

Ingredients

- 2 tablespoon of coconut butter
- ½ a cup of roasted red pepper chopped up
- 1 large sized finely chopped shallots
- 1 teaspoon of celery salt
- 1 tablespoon of seasoned salt
- 1 teaspoon of organic paprika
- 1 pinch of crushed red pepper flakes
- 4-5 cups of Cauliflower broken up into florets
- 4 cup of vegetable broth
- Just a splash of apple cider vinegar
- 1 pinch fresh thyme
- 1 cup of organic coconut milk

How To

1. Take a heavy bottomed pot and add coconut oil over medium heat
2. Add chopped up shallots and Saute for 3 minutes
3. Add chopped up and roasted pepper alongside the seasonings
4. Stir well and cook for 2-3 minutes
5. Add cauliflower, fresh thyme, and stock
6. Bring it to a simmer and cover the pot, cook for 5-10 minutes
7. Work in small batches and puree the soup using an immersion blender
8. Bring back the whole blended soup back to your pot and stir in coconut milk
9. Enjoy!

Nutrition Values (Per Serving)

- Calories: 171
- Fat: 16g
- Carbs: 7g
- Protein: 1g

Spiralized Asian Zucchini Salad

Serving: 10

Prep Time: 10 minutes

Cook Time: 0 minutes

Ingredients

- 1 thinly spiralized medium zucchini
- 1 pound of shredded cabbage
- 1 cup of sunflower seeds
- 1 cup of sliced almonds
- ¾ cup of avocado oil
- 1/3 cup of white vinegar
- 1 teaspoon of Stevia

How To

1. Cut up the spiralized zucchini into small portions using a kitchen knife

2. Take a large sized bowl and add sunflower seeds, cabbage, and almonds
3. Stir in zucchini
4. Take a small sized bowl and add oil, Stevia, and vinegar
5. Pour the dressing on top of the veggies and stir well
6. Chill for 2 hours and enjoy!

Nutrition Values (Per Serving)

- Calories: 120
- Fat: 10g
- Carbs: 7g
- Protein: 4g

Forever Together Courgette Salad

Prep Time: 20 minutes

Cooking Time: No cook required

Serving: 2

Ingredients

- Juice of 1 lemon
- 2 tablespoons of extra virgin olive oil
- ½ of a small pack of chopped up chives
- ½ of a small chopped up mint
- 300g of courgettes

Directions:

1. Take a large-sized bowl and pour lemon juice

2. Season with some salt and pepper

3. Whisk in olive oil and add the chopped up herbs

4. Put Courgette through a Spiralizer using the noodle attachment

5. Tip the zoodles to your bowl

6. Add the prepped salad dressing

7. Toss everything well

8. Serve and enjoy!

Nutrition Values (Per Serving)

- Calories: 144
- Fat: 12g
- Carbohydrates: 4g
- Protein: 4g

Roasted Cauliflower Soup

Serves: 6

Prep Time: 15 minutes

Cook Time: 60 minutes

Ingredients

- 2 cauliflower head broken up into florets
- Olive oil cooking spray
- ¼ cup of olive oil
- 1 chopped up a large onion
- 4 cloves of chopped up garlic
- 6 cups of water
- Salt as needed
- Pepper as needed

Directions

1. Add cauliflower florets to a large-sized bowl filled with salty water, wait for 20 minutes

2. Drain and arrange them on a sheet of aluminum foil on your baking sheet
3. Spray olive oil evenly over the cauliflower
4. Pre-heat your broiler to high and set the rack 6 inch away from the heat source
5. Broil for 20-30 minutes
6. Take a large soup pot and place it over medium heat
7. Add onion and cook for 5 minutes
8. Stir in garlic, roasted cauliflower and water and cook for 30 minutes
9. Blend the soup using an immersion blender and serve!

Nutritional Values per Serving

- Calories: 140
- Fat: 10g
- Carbohydrates: 11g
- Protein: 6g

Fine Vegan Pad Thai of Very Low Carb

Serving: 4

Prep Time: 15 minutes

Cook Time: 20 minutes

Ingredients

- 1 bag of Kelp noodles
- ½ cup of peanut butter
- 1 medium-sized white onion
- ¼ cup of Tamari
- Juice of 1 lime
- 3 cloves of garlic
- 2 teaspoon of red pepper flakes
- Shredded up carrots, chopped scallions, sesame seeds and cilantro

How To

1. Soak your noodles under water and allow them to wilt
2. Take a food processor and add peanut butter, tamari, onion, lime juice, garlic and pepper flakes
3. Process well
4. Drain the noodles and add ¼ of the sauce on top of the noodles
5. Give the whole mixture a toss
6. Serve with garnish and enjoy!

Nutrition Values (Per Serving)

- Calories: 231
- Fat: 16g
- Carbs: 7g
- Protein: 7g

Chapter 5: Dinner Recipes

Zucchini "Pizza" Boats

Prep Time: 10 minutes

Cooking Time: 25 minute

Serves: 4

Ingredients

- 4 pieces of medium zucchini
- ½ a cup Marinara sauce/tomato sauce
- 1/4 sliced red onion
- ¼ cup chopped kalamata olives
- ½ a cup of sliced cherry tomatoes

- 2 tablespoon of fresh basil

Directions

1. Pre-heat your oven to 400 degrees Fahrenheit
2. Cut up the Zucchini half-lengthwise and shape them in boats
3. Take a bowl and add Marinara/tomato sauce
4. Spread one layer of the sauce on top of each boat and top with onion, tomato, and olives
5. Bake for 20-25 minutes until the Zucchini are tender
6. Top with basil and serve!

Nutritional Values per Serving

- Calories: 278
- Fat: 20g
- Carbohydrates: 10g
- Protein: 15g

Clean Avocado Salad With Cilantro!

Prep Time: 10 minutes

Cooking Time: 0 minute

Serving: 6

Ingredients

- 2 avocados – peeled, pitted and diced
- 1 chopped up a sweet onion
- 1 green bell pepper (chopped up)
- 1 large sized chopped up red tomato
- ¼ cup of chopped up fresh cilantro
- ½ of a juiced lime
- Salt as needed
- Pepper as needed

How To

1. Take a medium-sized bowl and add onions, tomato, avocados, bell pepper, cilantro and lime juice
2. Mix well and coat everything well
3. Season with some salt and pepper
4. Serve chilled!

Nutrition Values (Per Serving)

- Calories: 126
- Fat: 10g
- Carbohydrates: 10g
- Protein: 2.1g

Mushroom and Pepper Kabob

Prep Time: 30 minutes

Cooking Time: 10 minute

Serves: 4

Ingredients

- ¾ cup of sliced fresh mushrooms
- 2 red bell peppers chopped up
- 1 green bell pepper cut up into 1-inch pieces
- ¼ cup of olive oil
- 2 tablespoon of lemon juice
- 1 minced garlic clove
- 2 teaspoon of chopped fresh thyme
- 1 teaspoon of chopped fresh rosemary
- ¼ teaspoon of salt
- ¼ teaspoon of ground black pepper

Directions

1. Pre-heat your grill to medium heat
2. Thread the mushroom and pepper alternately onto skewers
3. Take a small bowl and add olive oil, lemon juice, thyme, salt, pepper, rosemary and garlic
4. Brush the mushroom and pepper with the mixture
5. Brush the grate with oil
6. Place your kabobs on grill and cook for 4-6 minutes
7. Enjoy!

Nutritional Values per Serving

- Calories: 151
- Fat: 13g
- Carbohydrates: 6.5g
- Protein: 1.4g

Magical Mac and Cheese for Vegan Lovers

Serving: 4

Prep Time: 5 minutes

Cook Time: 50 minutes

Ingredients

For Vegan Cheese Sauce

- 1 cup of hemp sees
- ½ a cup of nutritional yeast
- ¼ cup chopped red pepper
- 1 teaspoon of salt
- ½ a teaspoon of onion powder
- ½ a teaspoon of garlic powder
- ½ -1 cup of water

For Macaroni

- 1 pack of Shirataki macaroni
- ¼ cup of the above-prepared sauce

How To

1. Pre-heat your oven to 350 degrees Fahrenheit
2. Take a blender and add the sauce ingredients and mix until smooth
3. You should have a queso like consistency
4. Rinse and drain your macaroni
5. Add the noodles and the sauce in the small sized baking dish and bake for about 45 minutes
6. Enjoy!

Nutrition Values (Per Serving)

- Protein: 18g
- Carbs: 5g
- Fats: 14g
- Calories: 286

Veggies With Chili And Almond

Prep Time: 10 minutes

Cooking Time: 10 hours *(Slow Cooker recipe)*

Serving: 6

Ingredients

- 2 tablespoon of olive oil
- 2 finely chopped onions
- 2 minced garlic cloves
- 1 finely sliced red bell pepper
- 1 finely sliced yellow bell pepper
- 2 cans of diced tomatoes
- 1 pack of frozen corn
- 1 cup of salsa sauce
- 1 teaspoon of paprika
- 1 teaspoon of salt
- Chopped up and toasted almonds as garnish
- Shredded Vegan Cheese

Directions

1. Take a large sized skillet and place it over high heat

2. Add olive oil and allow it to heat up

3. Add garlic and onions and Saute them until tender, add peppers and Saute again

4. Transfer the pepper and onion mix to your *Slow Cooker*

5. Add corn, tomatoes, and salsa sauce to the pot as well

6. Season with some paprika and salt

7. Cook on LOW for about 10 hours

8. Divide the mixture amongst serving bowls and scatter some almonds

9. Garnish with a bit of vegan cheese

10. Enjoy!

Nutrition Values per Serving

- Calories: 181
- Fat: 15g
- Carbohydrates: 10g
- Protein: 6g

Lovable Lo Mein

Serving: 4

Prep Time: 5 minutes

Cook Time: 10 minutes

Ingredients

- 1 pack of kelp noodles
- ¼ cup of julienned carrots
- ½ a cup of shelled Edamame
- ¼ cup of sliced mushrooms
- 1 cup of frozen spinach

For Sauce

- 2 tablespoon of tamari
- 1 tablespoon of sesame oil

- ½ a teaspoon of ground ginger
- ½ a teaspoon of garlic powder
- ¼ teaspoon of Sriracha

How To

1. Open your kelp noodle and soak them in water
2. Take a saucepan and place it over medium-low heat
3. Add sauce ingredients alongside veggie and Edamame
4. Add noodles after a while and cover it
5. Allow simmering for 4-5 minutes, making sure to keep stirring it from time to time
6. Add a few tablespoons of water if needed
7. Once the noodles are tender, mix everything well and remove the heat
8. Allow the noodle to sit for a while until the liquid has been absorbed
9. Serve and enjoy!

Nutrition Values (Per Serving)

- Protein: 8g
- Carbs: 5g
- Fats: 8g
- Calories: 139

Epic Mustard Dredged Brussels

Serving: 4

Prep Time: 15 minutes

Cook Time: 5 hours

Ingredients

- 1 pound of Brussels sprouts with the bottom trimmed off and cut
- 1 tablespoon of olive oil
- 1-1/2 a tablespoon of Dijon mustard
- ¼ cup of water
- Salt as needed
- Pepper as needed
- ½ a teaspoon of dried tarragon (optional)

Directions

1. Remove the lid of your pot and add water, mustard, and Brussels

2. Season them with some pepper, salt and tarragon if using

3. Stir the whole mixture well to ensure that the Brussels are coated properly

4. Cover and cook on LOW for about 5 hours until the Brussels are fork tender

5. Alternatively, you may cook a bit longer if you want slightly crispy Brussels

6. Give it a nice stir and serve!

<u>Nutrition Values per Serving</u>

- Calories: 83
- Fat: 4g
- Carbohydrates: 11g
- Protein: 4g

Very Proud Zucchini Saute!

Prep Time: 15 minutes

Cooking Time: 15 minute

Serving: 6

Ingredients

- 1 tablespoon of olive oil
- ½ of a diced red onion
- Salt as needed
- Pepper as needed
- 4 halved and sliced Zucchini
- ½ a pound of fresh sliced mushrooms
- 1 diced tomato
- 1 minced clove of garlic
- 1 teaspoon of Italian seasoning

How To

1. Take a large sized skillet and place it over medium heat
2. Add onion and Saute them for 2 minutes while seasoning them with some pepper and salt
3. Add Zucchini to skillet
4. Once the Zucchini is tender, add garlic, Italian seasoning, and tomatoes
5. Cook everything well
6. Enjoy!

Nutrition Values (Per Serving)

- Calories: 68
- Fat: 4g
- Carbohydrates: 10g
- Protein: 3g

Herbal Lemony Artichokes

Prep Time: 10 minutes

Cooking Time: 5 hours *(Slow Cooker recipe)*

Serving: 4

<u>Ingredients</u>:

- 5 large artichokes
- 1 teaspoon of fine sea salt
- 2 sliced stalks of celery
- 2 large sized carrots cut up into matchsticks
- Juice of ½ a fresh lemon
- ¼ teaspoon of black pepper
- 1 teaspoon of dried thyme
- 1 tablespoon of dried rosemary
- Lemon wedges for garnish

Directions

1. Remove the stalks of your artichoke and any tough outer leaves as well
2. Transfer the chokes to your *crock pot* and pour 2 cups of boiling water
3. Add celery, salt, lemon juice, carrots, black pepper, thyme, and rosemary
4. Cook for 4-5 hours on HIGH settings
5. Serve the chokes with lemon wedges

Nutrition Values per Serving

- Calories: 158
- Fat: 15g
- Carbohydrates: 5g
- Protein: 2g

Just Another Awesome Garlic Kale

Prep Time: 5 minutes

Cooking Time: 10 minutes

Serving: 4

Ingredients

- 1 bunch of kale
- 2 tablespoon of olive oil
- 4 minced garlic cloves

How To

1. Tear the kale into bite-sized portions by removing them from the thick stems
2. Discard the stems
3. Take a large sized pot and place it over medium heat
4. Add olive oil and allow it to heat up

5. Add garlic and stir for 2 minutes

6. Add kale and keep cooking for 5 minutes more

7. Enjoy!

Nutrition Values (Per Serving)

- Calories: 121
- Fat: 8g
- Carbohydrates: 10g
- Protein: 4g

Zucchini Pasta

Prep Time: 10 minutes

Cooking Time: 5 minutes

Serving: 1

Ingredients:

- 2 pieces of peeled Zucchini
- 1 tablespoon of extra virgin olive oil
- ¼ cup of water
- Salt as needed
- Ground black pepper as needed

Directions:

1. Cut the zucchini lengthwise using a veggie peeler (make sure to stop once you have reached the seeds)

2. Turn the Zucchini and keep peeling until all sides have been peeled up into long noodle-like strips of zoodles

3. Discard the seeds

4. Slice up the pieces into spaghetti-like strips

5. Take a skillet and place it over medium heat

6. Add olive oil and heat it up

7. Add zucchini to the hot oil and fry for about 1 minute

8. Add water and cook for 5-7 minutes until the Zucchini are tender

9. Season with some pepper and salt

10. Enjoy!

Nutrition Values (Per Serving)

- Calories: 157
- Fat: 13g
- Carbohydrates: 8g
- Protein: 3g

Sensual Fried Cakes

Serving: 12

Prep Time: 5 minutes

Cook Time: 10 minutes

Ingredients

- 1 can of palm hearts, drained and chopped up
- ½ a cup of vegan mayo
- 2 tablespoon of coconut flour
- 2 teaspoon of Psyllium Husk Fiber
- ¼ teaspoon of kelp flakes
- ¼ teaspoon of cayenne pepper
- 1 teaspoon of lemon juice
- Salt as needed
- Pepper as needed

How To

1. Take a frying pan and place it over medium-low heat

2. Take a mixing bowl and add all of the ingredients well and keep stirring them until a sturdy mixture form
3. Take the mixture and form them into patties
4. Add a bit of coconut flour if the texture seems too wet
5. Make small-sized cakes and cook them for about 5 minutes
6. Once the bottom shows a golden texture, flip them up and repeat for the other side
7. Enjoy!

Nutrition Values (Per Serving)

- Calories: 130
- Fat: 10g
- Carbs: 3g
- Protein: 1.5g

Garlic Chokes Slightly Charred Up

Prep Time: 5 minutes

Cooking Time: 30 minute

Serving: 4

Ingredients

- 2 large sized artichokes
- 1 quartered lemon
- ¾ cup of olive oil
- 4 chopped up garlic cloves
- 1 teaspoon of salt
- ½ a teaspoon of ground black pepper

How To

1. Take a large sized bowl and add water

2. Squeeze juice from the lemon wedge into the water

3. Trim the top of the chokes and cut them up into half lengthwise portions

4. Bring the water pot to boil

5. Pre-heat your outdoor grill to medium-high heat

6. Add artichokes to the boiling water and cook for 15 minutes

7. Drain them and squeeze the remaining lemon wedges into a medium sized bowl

8. Stir in garlic and olive oil

9. Season with some pepper and salt

10. Brush up the chokes with the coating of garlic dip and place them on your pre-heated grill

11. Grill up the chokes for about 10 minutes, making sure to keep basting them from time to time until the tips are slightly charred

12. Serve with the rest of the dips

Nutrition Values (Per Serving)

- Calories: 402
- Fat: 40g
- Carbohydrates: 10g
- Protein: 2.9g

Globe Trotting Evergreen Squash

Prep Time: 15 minutes

Cooking Time: 30 minutes

Serving: 4

Ingredients

- 2 tablespoon of vegetable oil
- 1 small sized sliced onion
- 2 medium-sized coarsely chopped tomatoes
- 1 teaspoon of salt
- ¼ teaspoon of pepper
- 2 small zucchini cut up into ½ inch slices
- 2 small sized yellow summer squash cut up into ½ inch slices
- 1 bay leaf
- ½ a teaspoon of dried basil

How To

1. Take a large sized skillet and place it over medium heat

2. Stir in onion and cook for 5 minutes
3. Add tomatoes and season with some salt and pepper
4. Keep cooking for 5 minutes
5. Add zucchini, yellow squash, bay leaf and basil and cover it up
6. Lower down the heat and allow it to simmer for 20 minutes making sure to keep stirring it
7. Discard the bay leaf and enjoy!

Nutrition Values (Per Serving)

- Calories: 65
- Fat: 5g
- Carbohydrates: 5g
- Protein: 1.5g

Chapter 6: Snack Recipes

Never Fear Thin Bagels Pieces

Serving: 8

Prep Time: 10 minutes

Cook Time: 40 minutes

Ingredients

- 3 tablespoon of ground flaxseed
- ½ a cup of tahini
- ½ a cup of Psyllium Husk powder
- 1 cup of water
- 1 teaspoon of baking powder
- Just a pinch of salt
- Sesame seeds for garnish

How To

1. Pre-heat your oven to 375 degrees Fahrenheit
2. Take a mixing bowl and add Psyllium Husk, baking powder, ground flax seeds, salt and keep whisking until combined
3. Add water to the dry mix and keep mixing until the water has been absorbed fully
4. Add tahini and keep mixing until the dough forms
5. Knead well
6. Form patties from the dough that have a diameter of 4 inches and a thickness of ¼ inch
7. Lay them carefully on your baking tray
8. Cut up a small hole in the middle
9. Add sesame seeds on top
10. Bake for 40 minutes until a golden brown texture is seen
11. Cut them in half and toast if you like
12. Top them up with your favorite Keto-Vegan compliant spread
13. Enjoy!

Nutrition Values (Per Serving)

- Calories: 129
- Fat: 10g
- Carbs: 2g
- Protein: 4g

Veggie Wraps With Glorious Tahini Sauce

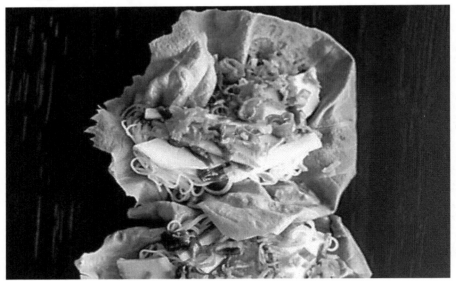

Serving: 8

Prep Time: 10 minutes

Cook Time: 0 minutes

Ingredients

- ¼ cup of sliced carrots
- 2 tablespoon of sauerkraut
- 2 tablespoon of tahini sauce

How To

1. De-vein your leaves and wash them well

2. Add carrots, sauerkraut and wrap them up well

3. Pour the sauce directly/use as a dip

4. Enjoy!

<u>Nutrition Values (Per Serving)</u>

- Calories: 120
- Fat: 8g
- Carbs: 6g
- Protein: 4g

Very White Chocolate Peanut Butter Bites

Serving: 8

Prep Time: 110 minutes

Cook Time: 0 minutes

Ingredients

- ½ a cup of cacao butter
- ½ a cup of salted peanut butter
- 3 tablespoon of Stevia
- 4 tablespoon of powdered coconut milk
- 2 teaspoon of vanilla extract

How To

1. Set your double boiler on low-heat
2. Melt the cacao butter and peanut butter together and stir in vanilla extract
3. Take another bowl and add powdered coconut powder and Stevia

4. Stir one tablespoon at a time of the mixture into the vanilla extract mixture
5. Portion the mixture into silicone molds or lined up muffin tins and chill them for 90 minutes
6. Remove and enjoy!

Nutrition Values (Per Serving)

- Calories: 77
- Fat: 7g
- Carbs: 8g
- Protein: 2g

Die Hard Crisp Breads for Keto Lovers

Serving: 20

Prep Time: 10 minutes

Cook Time: 75 minutes

Ingredients

- 1 cup of sesame seeds
- 1 cup of sunflower seeds
- 1 cup of flaxseeds
- ½ a cup of hulled hemp seeds
- 3 tablespoon of Psyllium Husk
- 1 teaspoon of salt
- 1 teaspoon of baking powder
- 2 cups of water

How To

1. Pre-heat your oven to a temperature of 350 degrees Fahrenheit

2. Take your blender and add seeds, baking powder, salt and Psyllium Husk
3. Blend well until a sand-like texture appears
4. Stir in water and mix until a batter forms
5. Allow the batter to rest for 10 minutes until a dough-like thick mixture form
6. Pour the dough onto cookie sheet lined up with parchment paper
7. Spread it evenly, making sure that it has a thickness of ¼ inch thick all around
8. Bake for 75 minutes in your oven
9. Remove and cut up into 20 spices
10. Allow them to cool for 30 minutes and enjoy!

Nutrition Values (Per Serving)

- Calories: 156
- Fat: 13g
- Carbs: 1g
- Protein: 5g

Very Inspiring Choke Salsa

Prep Time: 10 minutes

Cooking Time: 0 minute

Serving: 3

Ingredients

- 6.5 ounce of drained artichoke hearts (chopped)
- 3 chopped up plum tomatoes
- 2 tablespoon of chopped up red onion
- ¼ cup chopped up black olives
- 1 tablespoon of chopped up garlic
- 2 tablespoon of chopped up fresh basil
- Salt as needed
- Pepper as needed

How To

1. Take a medium-sized bowl and add hearts, tomatoes, onion, garlic pepper, olives, and salt
2. Toss well and serve!

Nutrition Values (Per Serving)

- Calories: 52
- Fat: 3g
- Carbohydrates: 7g
- Protein: 2g

Enjoyable Lemon Popsicles With Coconut

Serving: 6

Prep Time: 10 minutes

Cook Time: 120 minutes

Ingredients

- 3 and a ½ ounce of Raspberries
- Juice of ½ a lemon
- ¼ cup of coconut oil
- 1 cup of coconut milk
- ¼ cup of soy yogurt
- ¼ cup of coconut cream
- ½ a teaspoon of Guar Gum
- 20 drops of Liquid Stevia

How To

1. Take a bowl and add all of the ingredients

2. Use an immersion blender to mix everything well

3. Once done, pass the mixture through a mesh and strain them well, making sure to discard the raspberry seeds

4. Pour the mixture into a mold and chill for 2 hours

5. Pass the mold under hot water and dislodge the popsicles

6. Enjoy!

Nutrition Values (Per Serving)

- Protein: 0.5g
- Carbs: 2g
- Fats: 16g
- Calories: 150

Cauliflower Nuggets

Serving: 4

Prep Time: 10 minutes

Cook Time: 60 minutes

Ingredients

- 2 cups of cauliflower florets
- ¼ cup of chickpea flour
- 2 tablespoon of buffalo wing sauce
- ¼ cup of water

How To

1. Pre-heat your oven to 350 degrees Fahrenheit
2. Spread the florets out in a single layer in a pan and bake them in your oven for 30 minutes

3. During the final few minutes, take a bowl and add chickpea flour, water, sauce and mix well

4. Dip the florets in the batter and lay them back in the dish

5. Bake for 30 minutes more

6. Enjoy!

Nutrition Values (Per Serving)

- Protein: 5g
- Carbs: 10g
- Fats: 1g
- Calories: 80

Lemon Broccoli Platter

Serving: 6

Prep Time: 10 minutes

Cook Time: 15 minutes

Ingredients

- 2 heads of broccoli separated into florets
- 2 teaspoon of extra virgin olive oil
- 1 teaspoon of sea salt
- ½ a teaspoon of ground black pepper
- 1 minced garlic clove
- ½ a teaspoon of lemon juice

How To

1. Pre-heat your oven to a temperature of 400 degrees Fahrenheit

2. Take a large-sized bowl and add broccoli florets with some extra virgin olive oil, pepper, sea salt and garlic
3. Spread the broccoli out in a single layer on a fine baking sheet
4. Bake in your pre-heated oven for about 15-20 minutes until the florets are soft enough so that they can be pierced with a fork
5. Squeeze lemon juice over them generously before serving
6. Enjoy!

Nutrition Values (Per Serving)

- Calories: 49
- Fat: 2.9g
- Carbohydrates: 5g
- Protein: 2.9g

Mashed Cauliflower and Herbs

Serves: 4

Prep Time: 5 minutes

Cook Time: 3 hours *(Slow Cooker recipe)*

Ingredients

- 1 large sized cauliflower head
- 6 cloves of peeled garlic
- 4 tablespoon of minced herbs
- 1 cup of vegetable broth
- 4-6 cups of water
- 3 tablespoon of olive oil
- Salt as needed

Directions

1. Peel the leaves off your cauliflower and cut it up into medium sized florets

2. Add the florets to your *Slow Cooker* and top them up with vegetable broth, garlic cloves and water to submerge the cauliflowers
3. Cover and cook on HIGH for 3 hours
4. Drain the water and add the Cauliflower back to the cooker
5. Add olive oil and use immersion blender to mash the mixture
6. Season with some pepper and salt
7. Add the herbs to your mash and enjoy!

Nutrition Values per Serving

- Calories: 65
- Fat: 5g
- Carbohydrates: 5g
- Protein: 2g

Gentle Avocado Bowls

Serving: 1

Prep Time: 5 minutes

Cook Time: 0 minutes

Ingredients

For Dressing

- ¼ cup of extra virgin olive oil
- ¼ cup of lemon juice
- 1 tablespoon of poppy seeds
- 1 teaspoon of grated ginger
- ¼ teaspoon of salt

For Else

- 1 medium-sized Hass avocado
- 1 small sized shredded carrot

- 2 tablespoon of tahini

How To

1. Take a sealing jar and add dressing ingredients, shake it well
2. Take a separate dish and add 2 tablespoons of dressing alongside grated carrot
3. Cut up the avocado in half and remove the pit
4. Spoon the dressed carrots into the avocado halves
5. Drizzle tahini all over
6. Enjoy!

Nutrition Values (Per Serving)

- Protein: 8g
- Carbs: 5g
- Fats: 52g
- Calories: 562

Healthy Low-Carb Green Smoothie

Serving: 1

Prep Time: 5 minutes

Cook Time: 5 minutes

Ingredients

- 2 cups of spinach
- 1 and a ½ cups of ice
- 1 cup of almond milk
- ½ of an avocado, chopped and pitted
- 1/4 cup of vegan protein powder
- ¼ cup of stevia

How To

1. Add almond milk, spinach and any remaining ingredients to the blender
2. Blend until you have a nice texture
3. Add a bit of ice and stir
4. Pour into large glasses and serve!

Nutrition Values (Per Serving)

- Calories: 165
- Fat: 5g
- Carbs: 10g
- Protein: 29g

Crazy Cinnamon and Almond Butter Smoothie

Serving: 1

Prep Time: 2 minutes

Cook Time: 0 minutes

Ingredients

- 1 and a ½ cups of almond milk
- 1 scoop of collagen peptides
- 2 tablespoon of almond butter
- 2 tablespoon of golden flax meal
- ½ a teaspoon of cinnamon
- 15 drops of liquid stevia
- 1/8 teaspoon of almond extract
- 1/8 teaspoon of salt
- 6-8 ice cubes

How To

1. Add all of the ingredients to your blender and blend well until smooth
2. Allow them it to chill and enjoy!

Nutrition Values (Per Serving)

- Calories: 326
- Fat: 27g
- Carbs: 11g
- Protein: 19g

Pumpkin Scones, Low Carb

Serving: 1

Prep Time: 5 minutes

Cook Time: 40 minutes

Ingredients

- ½ a cup of coconut flour
- ¼ cup of salted vegan butter
- 6 tablespoon of vegan yogurt
- 6 tablespoon of pumpkin puree
- 2 Whole "Flax Eggs"
- 2 tablespoon of Swerve
- 2 teaspoon of pumpkin pie spice

How To

1. Pre-heat your oven to 350 degrees Fahrenheit
2. Take a mixing bowl and add spices, coconut flour and swerve
3. Cut the vegan butter into the mix and keep forking until crumbly mixture appears
4. Add pumpkin puree and yogurt and mix well
5. Add flax eggs one by one and mix well
6. Scoop up the mixture into a tray and bake for about 40 minutes until finely browned
7. Remove and enjoy!

Nutrition Values (Per Serving)

- Protein: 8g
- Carbs: 5g
- Fats: 52g
- Calories: 562

A Song of Watermelon and Ice

Prep Time: 15 minutes

Cooking Time: 0 minute

Serving: 3

Ingredients

- 3 cups of chopped up watermelon
- ½ a cup of chopped up green bell pepper
- 2 tablespoon of lime juice
- 2 tablespoon of chopped fresh cilantro
- 1 tablespoon of chopped green onions
- 1 tablespoon of chopped jalapeno
- ½ a teaspoon of garlic salt

How To

1. Take a large sized bowl and add lime juice, watermelon, green bell pepper, garlic salt, green onion, cilantro and jalapeno

2. Mix well and toss the whole mixture

3. Serve the salad chilled up!

Nutrition Values (Per Serving)

- Calories: 52
- Fat: 5g
- Carbohydrates: 1.3g
- Protein: 1g

Brussels Sprouts Chips

Serving: 4

Prep Time: 10 minutes

Cook Time: 10-15 minutes

Ingredients

- 1 pound of Brussels, washed and dried
- 2 tablespoon of extra virgin olive oil
- 1 teaspoon of kosher salt

How To

1. Pre-heat your oven to 400 degrees Fahrenheit
2. Prepare the sprouts by trimming the stock and peels
3. Discard the outer leaves one by one all the way to the core
4. Transfer the leaves to a bowl

5. Add oil to the leaves and toss them well to coat them

6. Season with salt and pepper

7. Spread them evenly on baking sheet, making sure to spread the leaves

8. Bake for 10-15 minutes until deep brown

9. Remove from oven and allow them to cool

10. Sprinkle a bit of salt and serve

Nutrition (Per Serving)

- Protein: 3g
- Carbs: 5g
- Fats: 7g
- Calories: 104

Chapter 7: Dessert Recipes

Tantalizing Apple Pie Bites

Serving: 4

Prep Time: 20 minutes

Cook Time: 0 minutes

Ingredients

- 1 cup chopped walnuts
- ½ a cup of coconut oil
- ¼ cup of ground flaxseed
- ½ ounce of frozen dried apples
- 1 teaspoon of vanilla extract
- 1 teaspoon of cinnamon
- Liquid Stevia

How To

1. Melt the coconut oil until it is liquid

2. Take your blender and add walnuts, coconut oil, and process well
3. Add flaxseeds, vanilla, and Stevia
4. Keep processing until a fine mixture form
5. Stop and add crumbled dried apples
6. Process until your desired texture appears
7. Portion the mixture amongst muffin molds and allow them to chill
8. Enjoy!

Nutrition Values (Per Serving)

- Calories: 194
- Fat: 19g
- Carbs: 2g
- Protein: 2.3g

Vegan Compliant Protein Balls

Serving: 8

Prep Time: 20 minutes

Cook Time: 0 minutes

Ingredients

- 1 cup of creamed coconut
- 2 scoops of Vega Sport Chocolate Protein (or any protein powder of your preference)
- ¼ cup of ground flax seed
- ½ a teaspoon of vanilla extract
- ½ a teaspoon of mint extract
- 1-2 tablespoon of cocoa powder

How To

1. Take a large sized bowl and melt the creamed coconut
2. Add the vanilla extract and stir well

3. Stir in flax seed, protein powder and knead until the fine dough forms
4. Form 24 balls and allow the balls to chill for 10-15 minutes
5. Roll them up in some cocoa powder if you prefer and serve!

Nutrition Values (Per Serving)

- Calories: 260
- Fat: 20g
- Carbs: 3g
- Protein: 10g

The Keto Lovers "Magical" Grain Free Granola

Serving: 10

Prep Time: 10 minutes

Cook Time: 75 minutes

Ingredients

- ½ a cup of raw sunflower seeds
- ½ a cup of raw hemp hearts
- ½ a cup of flaxseeds
- ¼ cup of chia seeds
- 2 tablespoon of Psyllium Husk powder
- 1 tablespoon of cinnamon
- Stevia
- ½ a teaspoon of baking powder
- ½ a teaspoon of salt
- 1 cup of water

How To

1. Pre-heat your oven to 300 degrees Fahrenheit
2. Line up a baking sheet with parchment paper
3. Take your food processor and grind all the seeds
4. Add the dry ingredients and mix well
5. Stir in water until fully incorporated
6. Allow the mixture to sit for a while until it thickens up
7. Spread the mixture evenly on top of your baking sheet (giving a thickness of about ¼ inch)
8. Bake for 45 minutes
9. Break apart the granola and keep baking for another 30 minutes until the pieces are crunchy
10. Remove and allow them to cool
11. Enjoy!

Nutrition Values (Per Serving)

- Calories: 292
- Fat: 25g
- Carbs: 12g
- Protein: 8g

Pumpkin Butter Nut Cup

Serves: 5

Prep Time: 135 minutes

Cook Time: 0 minute

For Filing

- ½ a cup of organic pumpkin puree
- 1/2a cup of almond butter
- 4 tablespoon of organic coconut oil
- ¼ teaspoon of organic ground nutmeg
- ¼ teaspoon of organic ground ginger
- 1 teaspoon of organic ground cinnamon
- 1/8 teaspoon of organic ground clove
- 2 teaspoon of organic vanilla extract

For Topping

- 1 cup of organic raw cacao powder
- 1 cup of organic coconut oil

Directions

1. Take a medium-sized bowl and add all of the listed ingredients under pumpkin filling
2. Mix well until you have a creamy mixture
3. Take another bowl and add the topping mixture and mix well
4. Take a muffin cup and fill it up with 1/3 of the chocolate topping mix
5. Chill for 15 minutes
6. Add 1/3 of the pumpkin mix and layer out on top
7. Chill for 2 hours
8. Repeat until all the mixture has been used up
9. Enjoy!

Nutritional Values per Serving

- Calories: 105
- Fat: 10.1g
- Carbohydrates: 3.3g
- Protein: 2.9g

Unique Gingerbread Muffins

Serving: 12

Prep Time: 15 minutes

Cook Time: 30 minutes

Ingredients

- 1 tablespoon of ground flaxseed
- 6 tablespoon of coconut milk
- 1 tablespoon of apple cider vinegar
- ½ a cup of peanut butter
- 2 tablespoon of gingerbread spice blend
- 1 teaspoon of baking powder
- 1 teaspoon of vanilla extract
- 2-3 tablespoon of Swerve

How To

1. Pre-heat your oven to a temperature of 350 degrees Fahrenheit
2. Take a bowl and add flaxseeds, sweetener, salt, vanilla, spices and coconut milk
3. Keep it on the side for a while
4. Add peanut butter, baking powder and keep mixing until combined well
5. Stir in peanut butter and baking powder
6. Mix well
7. Spoon the mixture into muffin liners
8. Bake for 30 minutes
9. Allow them to cool and enjoy!

Nutrition Values (Per Serving)

- Calories:158
- Fat: 13g
- Carbs: 3g
- Protein: 6g

The Vegan Pumpkin Spicy Fat Bombs

Serving: 12

Prep Time: 100 minutes

Cook Time: 0 minutes

Ingredients

- ¾ cup of pumpkin puree
- ¼ cup of hemp seeds
- ½ a cup of coconut oil
- 2 teaspoon of pumpkin pie spice
- 1 teaspoon of vanilla extract
- Liquid Stevia

How To

1. Take a blender and add all of the ingredients
2. Blend them well and portion the mixture out into silicon molds
3. Allow them to chill and enjoy!

Nutrition Values (Per Serving)

- Calories: 103
- Fat: 10g
- Carbs: 2g
- Protein: 1g

The Low Carb "Matcha" Bombs

Serving: 12

Prep Time: 100 minutes

Cook Time: 0 minutes

Ingredients

- ¾ cup of hemp sees
- ½ a cup of coconut oil
- 2 tablespoon of coconut butter
- 1 teaspoon of matcha powder
- 2 tablespoon of vanilla extract
- ½ a teaspoon of mint extract
- Liquid Stevia

How To

1. Take your blender and add hemp seeds, matcha, coconut oil, mint extract and Stevia
2. Blend well and divide the mixture into silicon molds
3. Melt the coconut butter and drizzle them on top of your cups
4. Allow the cups to chill and serve!

Nutrition Values (Per Serving)

- Calories: 200
- Fat: 20g
- Carbs: 3g
- Protein: 5g

The No-Bake Keto Cheese Cake

Serving: 4

Prep Time: 120 minutes

Cook Time: 0 minutes

Ingredients

For Crust

- 2 tablespoon of ground flaxseed
- 2 tablespoon of desiccated coconut
- 1 teaspoon of cinnamon

For Filling

- 4 ounce of vegan cream cheese
- 1 cup of soaked cashews
- ½ a cup of frozen blueberries
- 2 tablespoon of coconut oil
- 1 tablespoon of lemon juice

- 1 teaspoon of vanilla extract
- Liquid Stevia

How To

1. Take a container and mix all of the crust ingredients
2. Mix them well and flatten them at the bottom to prepare the crust
3. Take a blender and mix all of the filling ingredients and blend until smooth
4. Distribute the filling on top of your crust and chill it in your freezer for about 2 hours
5. Enjoy!

Nutrition Values (Per Serving)

- Calories: 182
- Fat: 16g
- Carbs: 6g
- Protein: 3g

Raspberry Chocolate Cups

Serving: 12

Prep Time: 60 minutes

Cook Time: 0 minutes

Ingredients

- ½ a cup of cacao butter
- ½ a cup of coconut manna
- 4 tablespoon of powdered coconut milk
- 3 tablespoon of granulated sugar substitute
- 1 teaspoon of vanilla extract
- ¼ cup of dried and crushed frozen raspberries

How To

1. Melt cacao butter and add coconut manna
2. Stir in vanilla extract
3. Take another dish and add coconut powder and sugar substitute

4. Stir the coconut mix into the cacao butter, 1 tablespoon at a time, making sure to keep mixing after each addition
5. Add the crushed dried raspberries
6. Mix well and portion it out into muffin tins
7. Chill for 60 minutes and enjoy!

Nutrition Values (Per Serving)

- Calories: 158
- Fat: 15g
- Carbs: 1g
- Protein: 3g

Exuberant Pumpkin Fudge

Serving: 25

Prep Time: 120 minutes

Cook Time: 0 minutes

Ingredients

- 1 and a ¾ cup of coconut butter
- 1 cup of pumpkin puree
- 1 teaspoon of ground cinnamon
- ¼ teaspoon of ground nutmeg
- 1 tablespoon of coconut oil

How To

1. Take an 8x8 inch square baking pan and line it with aluminum foil to start with

2. Take a spoon of the coconut butter and add into a heated pan; let the butter melt over low heat

3. Toss in the spices and pumpkin and keep stirring it until a grainy texture has formed

4. Pour in the coconut oil and keep stirring it vigorously in order to make sure that everything is combined nicely

5. Scoop up the mixture into the previously prepared baking pan and distribute evenly

6. Place a piece of wax paper over the top of the mixture and press on the upper side to make evenly straighten up the topside

7. Remove the wax paper and throw it away

8. Place the mixture in your fridge and let it cool for about 1-2 hours

9. Take it out and cut it into slices, then eat

Nutrition Values (Per Serving)

- Calories: 120
- Protein: 1.2g
- Carbs: 4.2g
- Fats: 10.7g

Conclusion

I would like to thank you for purchasing this book and taking the time to go through the book as well.

I do hope that this book has been helpful and you found the information contained in the publication useful!

Keep in mind that you are not only limited to the recipes provided in this book! Just go ahead and keep on exploring until you create your very own culinary masterpiece!

Stay healthy and stay safe!

Made in the USA
Lexington, KY
21 June 2019